PREPARATION FOR
THE IOWA TEST
OF BASIC SKILLS®
GRADE 3 READING COACH

by Vivienne Hodges, Ph.D.
and Stuart Margulies, Ph.D.

Educational Design, Inc.

Table of Contents

Introduction to the Teacher

This book is aimed at the development of higher-order reading competencies for third-grade students. It prepares students for the Iowa Test of Basic Skills (ITBS), which taps a wide variety of conceptual levels, ranging from the lowest level (constructing factual meaning) through the inferential/interpretive level to the critical/evaluative level.

The student typically reads a selection and then answers a multiple-choice question with four answer choices. Selections on the ITBS range from simple to difficult. The item types are drawn from all levels—simple recall, constructing meaning, and evaluating meaning. The largest number of items require students to construct inferential and evaluative meaning, and the instructional strategies emphasized most heavily in *The ITBS Reading Coach* are aimed at developing the competencies tapped by these higher levels.

Most teachers use *The Coach* by having their students proceed straight through the book. At the end, students take two practice tests, the first of which is followed by a lengthy discussion of answers. Another common way to use *The Coach* is to begin by giving students the first practice test. The teacher can use the results of this test to diagnose the areas requiring the most work. Sometimes a student reads only those units in which he or she needs further work.

Selections included in this book match ITBS Reading Comprehension item profiles. They have been chosen for their high interest level. Students benefit most when they can read the stories at a relaxed pace and have plenty of time for classroom discussion.

We hope and expect not only that students will enhance their reading competencies and do better on the ITBS, but that they will also enjoy the reading selections.

Introduction to the Student

This book, *The ITBS Reading Coach*, will help you read better. It will also help you do well on the ITBS Reading Test by showing you how to answer the types of questions you will find on this test.

At the end of the book are two Practice Tests. The first one is followed by a discussion of the answers. The second is not.

Both Practice Tests are like the ITBS Test. They will help you to get ready to do your best on the test.

PART 1:
Factual Meaning

In this part of the ITBS Reading Coach, you will read many short reading selections. After each selection, there is a question about it. You must pick out the correct answer from these answer choices. Only one of the answers is correct, so you have to be careful when you pick.

You have to read these selections carefully, too. The answers to the questions are right there in the selections. If you really understand what you have read, you will find the questions easy to answer.

1 Recalling Stated Information

Many questions on the ITBS Reading Test ask you to find a fact or a detail. You must then check back in the reading passage to make sure you get the right answer.

❖ Example 1

> Food energy is measured in calories. A large pear has 125 calories. A regular hamburger has 350 calories. A slice of cake with whipped cream has about 600 calories. An average piece of pie has only 400 calories.

1 **Which has the most calories?**

A A large pear
B A slice of birthday cake with whipped cream
C A typical hamburger
D An average slice of pie

The correct answer is **B**. You need to check back in the selection to see which food has the most calories.

The next example is also about things you eat. Remember, you can find the answer right there in the selection.

3 1833 04050 9942

❖ Example 2

> Many Americans eat very little for breakfast. Some have tea or coffee when they wake up. They wait until 1 or 2 in the afternoon for their first meal. Others have just a small roll in the morning. Some like a glass of juice as soon as they wake up.

2 **What kind of breakfast do many Americans have?**

    A A very large one
    B A very small one
    C Bacon and eggs
    D Coffee and Danish

The correct answer is **B**. Many Americans eat a very small breakfast. You can't find the other information in this selection.

Sequence

A selection often tells the order in which things happen. Words like before and after, or first and last, tell you the order, or sequence, in which things happen.

Read the next example. Decide when people stopped sitting near Amanda.

❖ Example 3

> Everyone liked Amanda when she first came to school. Even after she had a fight with Nancy, we still liked her. But after she started shooting rubber bands at everyone, she became a big pest. Now no one sits near her. Even her cousin Tommy doesn't want to be her friend anymore.

3 **People stopped sitting near Amanda**

    A after she first came to school.
    B after she hit Nancy.
    C after she started shooting rubber bands.
    D after Tommy stopped being friendly with her.

The correct answer is **C, after she started shooting rubber bands.**

Read each of the following selections. Look carefully at the facts given. Check to make sure before you choose your answer.

Helpful Hints
for Finding STATED INFORMATION
and UNDERSTANDING SEQUENCE

1. Any time you read, pay attention to facts and figures.

2. If you are asked a question about a fact, check back in the selection.

3. If you must decide the order in which things happen, look for key words such as first, last, before, and after.

SELECTIONS FOR PRACTICE

✳ Selection 1

> The Civil War began in 1861. It ended in 1865. World War I ended in 1918. America entered World War II in 1941. World War II ended in 1945.

1 **When did World War II end?**

    A 1861
    B 1918
    C 1941
    D 1945

✳ Selection 2

The highest ranking officer in the army is a general. Colonels are next in rank below generals. A lieutenant is a lower officer. A private is at the lowest rank in the army.

2 **Colin Powell was the highest-ranking officer in the army. He was**

A a colonel.
B a general.
C a lieutenant.
D a private.

✳ Selection 3

The Best Comic Shop sells old comics. They sell an old Spider Man comic for $20 and an old Zap Comix for $30. One of the first Archie comics costs $150. An early Superman costs $3,000.

3 **Early Archie comic books cost**

A $20.
B $30.
C $150.
D $3,000.

✳ Selection 4

Harriet Beecher Stowe wrote a great book about slavery. It made Americans realize how badly slaves were treated. Harriet Tubman was an African American woman who used to be a slave. She helped many slaves escape into freedom.

Amelia Earhart was a famous woman flyer. And Georgia O'Keefe is one of America's favorite painters.

4 **Who was a great writer?**

A Amelia Earhart
B Georgia O'Keefe
C Harriet Beecher Stowe
D Harriet Tubman

✳ Selection 5

A new drug must first be tested on laboratory animals. Then it can be tried on a dozen people. If that works well, it can be tested on a few hundred people. If this larger test works well, it can be used by everyone. It takes a long time to test a drug.

5 **When is a new drug tried on laboratory animals?**

A   after a hundred people have used it.
B   after it works well on a dozen people.
C   before it is tried on a dozen people.
D   if it works well on a large number of people.

✳ Selection 6

Mr. Jason is our music teacher. Last month he won first prize in a music quiz on TV. He was asked a lot of questions about music. He got all the questions right, and his answers made people laugh. Everyone in our class watched the program.

After he won the prize, Mr. Jason started his classes in a new way. Now he sings funny songs. He waits until everyone laughs and the class relaxes. Then he plays music.

6 **How does Mr. Jason get his class to listen to music?**

A   By singing funny songs
B   By playing rock music on the radio
C   By starting his class early
D   By being very strict with his students

2 Working Out What Words Mean

As you read, you may come across a word you don't know. You may be able to figure out what the word means by seeing how it is used.

> That is artificial ice cream.

Do you know what "artificial" means? You can't figure it out from this sentence. But you can figure out what it means if you read the whole paragraph.

> That is artificial ice cream. It doesn't have any real cream in it. It is made from fish and plants. It doesn't taste nearly as good as real ice cream.

Have you figured out what "artificial" means? "Artificial" means fake or not real. The second sentence gave a good clue. "It doesn't have real cream in it." "Real" is the opposite of "artificial."

Look at how a new word is used. Look at the other words in the sentence. Look at the sentences before and after the new words. This is called the context.

Read the next example and figure out the meaning of the word "savage" from the context.

❖ Example 1

> Frank acts like a savage in the lunchroom. He grabs food. He eats with his hands. He won't use a knife and fork. And he pushes people so he can get to the front of the line.

1 A "savage" is

A a friend.
B a wild person.
C an honest person.
D a shy person.

The correct choice is **B, a wild person**. You read how Frank acted. He doesn't act like a friend. He doesn't act like a shy person or an honest person. He is a wild man. You figured out what savage means from the context.

Try the next example.

❖ Example 2

> Rashan thinks the stars are beautiful. He can gaze at them for an hour. He likes to visit his uncle in the country. The sky is as black as soot there, so he can really see the stars well.

2 **A person who "gazes" at the stars**

    A dislikes them.
    B draws them.
    C looks at them.
    D talks to them.

The correct choice is **C, looks at them**. Rashan can look at the stars for an hour. He likes to go to the country to look at the stars when it's dark. To "gaze" means to look at something with a lot of interest.

Phrases

Sometimes you must figure out what a phrase of two or more words means. Read Example 3 and figure out the meaning of "accurate shooter."

❖ Example 3

> Most basketball players are tall. Bunny Levitt was very short. But Bunny was a good shot. He almost never missed. He could throw a ball into the basket almost every time.
>
> In 1935, there was a contest. Bunny threw the ball into the basket 499 times. He was the most accurate shooter who ever lived. He didn't miss once. No one today is as good a shooter as Bunny was.

3 An "accurate shooter"

    A likes to play basketball.

    B almost never misses.

    C must be tall.

    D can run very fast.

The correct answer is **B, almost never misses**. The selection tells us that Bunny almost never missed throwing the ball into the basket. The story told us Bunny wasn't tall. It didn't say whether Bunny could run fast or liked to play basketball.

Now read the following selections and decide what the new vocabulary words mean.

Helpful Hints
for Figuring Out the Meaning of a New Word or Phrase

1. Read the sentence with the new word or phrase.

2. Read the sentences before and after this word or phrase.

3. Guess what the word means from the context.

4. Look at the answers. Pick the choice closest to what you guessed.

SELECTIONS FOR PRACTICE

✳ Selection 1

> Bob joined the army. He packed up all his clothes. He said good-bye to all his friends. Then he had one final responsibility to take care of before he left. He brought his cat Carmen to his cousin's house. When that final job was done, he was ready to go into the army.

1 A "responsibility" is

   A something you can wear.
   B something you like a lot.
   C something you are supposed to do.
   D something you never want to do.

✳ Selection 2

> We listened to a debate on the radio. It was about our schools. Some of the people said that schools should be open during the summer. They think we need to learn a lot more than we do. They say there isn't enough time during the school year to learn what we need to know. Other people said that it's important to close schools during the summer. They say students and teachers need to take a break.

2 When people are in a "debate," they

   A give their opinions about a subject they disagree on.
   B learn a lot more than usual in school.
   C listen carefully to the radio.
   D take a break after doing hard work.

✳ Selection 3

> We heard this incredible story from Tomas. He said two people came to his house last night. They each had big heads and eyes that glowed in the dark. They said they came from another world. They told Tomas he was going to be king of this other world.

3 An "incredible" story is

A boring.
B hard to believe.
C sad.
D very long.

✳ Selection 4

> Mr. and Mrs. Grande always observe the law. They always stop at red lights. They always wear seat belts when they are in the car. They try to do what the laws say they should do.

4 A person who "observes the law"

A doesn't pay attention to the law.
B doesn't understand the law.
C often breaks the law.
D tries to follow the law.

NOTICE: Photocopying any part of this book is forbidden by law.

19

✳ Selection 5

> I watched a long TV program about England. The narrator was the Queen. She described all the scenes the TV was showing. She also told us that it is a hard job to be the Queen. I thought it would be fun, but it seems that it isn't enjoyable. People look at you all the time. You never have time for yourself.

5 A "narrator" is

A   a person who is very rich.

B   the person who describes what is happening.

C   a very happy person.

D   a very poor man or woman.

✳ Selection 6

> His name was Francesco Lentini. He was born almost 100 years ago. He was like everybody else except for one thing. Francesco had three legs.
>
> When Francesco was a child, he could run on all three legs. But when he was a mature adult, he ran on two legs. His third leg was too short to reach the ground.

6 A "mature adult" is

A   one or two days old.

B   less than one year old.

C   about six years old.

D   18 years old or older.

PART 2:
Inferring Meaning

In Part 1 of the ITBS Reading Coach, you answered questions by finding information stated in the selection. In the rest of the Coach, the answer is NOT stated in the selection. You must figure it out for yourself.

3 Making Inferences and Drawing Conclusions

Suppose you see two fire trucks in front of a building and you smell smoke. You would figure out that there was probably a fire. Nobody has to tell you. You could make a good guess.

We call this "making an inference." You inferred that there was a fire in the building based on what you saw and smelled.

Read Example 1. Figure out what is happening to Fred in the story.

❖ Example 1

> Fred coughed. Then he sneezed. His head hurt. His mother said he had a fever. She told him to go to bed and gave him some juice to drink. Fred stayed home and slept. He felt terrible.

1 **What do you think was wrong with Fred?**

   A He was feeling nervous.
   B He had a bad cold.
   C He was tired from playing too much.
   D He ate too much.

The correct answer is **B**. You cough and sneeze when you have a bad cold.

In this example, you read that Fred was coughing and sneezing. This helped you to infer, or conclude that Fred had a bad cold.

Read the next passage. At the end, you will be asked to draw a conclusion about what you have read.

❖ Example 2

> Six hundred years ago books cost a lot. Only rich people owned them. Few people even knew how to read.
>
> In those days, books were not printed. They were written by hand. It could take a year to copy all the pages in a book. That's why books cost so much back then.
>
> Today, books are made quickly. A printing press can print 10,000 books a day. There are books about everything.

2 **What has changed in the last 600 years?**

   A Fewer people know how to read today.
   B Books cost more today.
   C Only rich people buy books.
   D There are more people today who can read.

Again, you must draw a conclusion from what you read. You must decide how books (or the people who read them) have changed. The correct answer is **D**. There are many more books around today, and that must mean that many more people can read them.

Setting

A story's setting is where and when it takes place. Sometimes the author will name the setting. Sometimes you must figure out for yourself where a story is set.

Read the next story and decide where it takes place.

❖ Example 3

> First Saretha got some milk. Then she got lettuce, carrots, and potatoes. She spent a long time picking out the ice cream. Finally she chose vanilla. She really prefers strawberry, but her brother hates it.

3 **The story is set**

    A on a beach.
    B at a circus.
    C at a movie.
    D in a food store.

The correct answer is **D**. The story is set in a food store. You have several clues that tell you this. You are told that Saretha got milk. Then she got lettuce, carrots, and potatoes. She also got ice cream. A food store is the only choice that makes sense. You can buy food at the movies, or when you go to the beach or the circus, but you can't get all these different kinds of food there.

A story can take place in winter or summer. It may be set 1,000 years ago, or today, or next week. It may be set in the morning or at night.

Read Example 4 and decide when it is set.

❖ Example 4

> Most of the buildings were dark. Some still had lights on, but only in a few rooms. There were a few cars still on the road, and their headlights lit up the whole street. The city was quiet.

4   **What time was it?**

   A   about 9 A.M.
   B   about 12 noon
   C   about 3 in the afternoon
   D   late at night

D is the correct choice. Late at night it gets very quiet. None of the other choices could be correct. There is daylight at 9 A.M., 12 noon, and 3 in the afternoon. It is clearly after dark in the story.

Helpful Hints
for MAKING INFERENCES from what you read

1. When you are asked to make an inference, you must make a good guess. You won't find the correct answer in the story.

2. Read the passage. Then read the question. Decide what you think the answer should be. Then look at the choices. Make the best choice you can. even if you are not sure of the answer.

3. Find clues to tell you where the story takes place and when things happen.

SELECTIONS FOR PRACTICE

✳ Selection 1

> José, Leroy, and Sanjae all took up weightlifting. At first they worked out for a half hour every Monday, Wednesday, and Friday. But now that they've been doing it for a few months, they work out for an hour every day. One thing they all notice is that their clothes feel very tight. They all need to wear bigger shirts.

1 **What might you conclude?**

A José, Leroy, and Sanjae are wearing the wrong kind of shirt.
B José, Leroy, and Sanjae are getting sick from lifting weights.
C José, Leroy, and Sanjae now have bigger chests and more muscles.
D José, Leroy, and Sanjae should change to another sport.

✳ Selection 2

> One corner of the room looked like a forest. It was filled with soft animals. I saw a green monkey and a pink elephant and lots and lots of orange lions and tigers.
>
> The rest of the room was quite different. It was filled with tall shelves. One set of shelves had board games—Chutes and Ladders, Monopoly, Scrabble, Chess, Checkers. The shelves against the wall were filled with cars and trucks and fire engines.

2 **Where does the story take place?**

A In an office building
B In a small park
C In a toy store
D At a zoo

Jackie loved her snake Sam. But it's hard having a snake for a pet. Some people are afraid of snakes. Jackie's mother wasn't afraid. However, she wished Sam lived somewhere else. Jackie loved her pet, but she wanted her mother to be happy, too.

Then Mr. Smith said he would keep Sam in the school zoo. He would feed Sam and keep his cage clean. Jackie was sad, but she was pleased, too.

3 **Why was Jackie pleased when Mr. Smith said Sam could live in the school zoo?**

  A She wanted Mr. Smith to see that Sam was a great pet.
  B She was afraid of snakes.
  C She knew it would make her mom happy.
  D She was tired of having Sam for a pet.

4 Making Generalizations and Applying Information

You have just learned how to make inferences. Now you will take that one step further. You will learn how to make a generalization based on an inference.

In your life, you've seen lots of cats and dogs. And so, you know about how big cats are and about how big dogs are. You know that, in general, dogs are bigger than cats. A statement like "dogs are bigger than cats" is called a generalization.

Let's start with a simple inference. Read the passage about Kisha and make an inference based on the information you read.

❖ Example 1

> Kisha had an exciting day. Her sister woke her at 7 A.M. to give her her gift. There was a party for her in school. And just before she went to bed her father promised her a new puppy.

1A **Why do you think so many good things happened to Kisha?**

    A It was the first day of summer.
    B It was Christmas Day.
    C It was her birthday.
    D It was the day she started school.

Choice C is correct. People give us gifts and parties for our birthday.

The next question asks you to make a generalization based on this passage and on what you know about birthdays.

1B **You have learned what happened to Kisha on her birthday. What might you guess about birthdays in general?**

    A They are happy days for the birthday boy or girl.
    B They are sad for people who are not having birthdays.
    C They cost a very great deal of money.
    D They happen very seldom.

Choice A is correct. You read in this story that Kisha was given gifts and a party on her birthday. You can generalize from this, and from what you know about other birthdays, that birthdays are happy days.

Sometimes you must make an inference based on a passage. Then you must apply this inference to a different situation.

❖ Example 2

> Lions and sharks are carnivorous. This means that they eat other animals for food. Most plants are not carnivorous, but a very few are. The Venus's-flytrap is a plant that eats insects. It has leaves that snap shut like a trap when an insect lands on them. The insect cannot get out and is slowly eaten by the plant.

2 **The pitcher plant is another carnivorous plant. What would you guess it feeds on?**

    A Air
    B Bugs
    C Grass
    D Soil

You learned that carnivorous plants eat living creatures for their food. The question told you that the pitcher plant is carnivorous. Then it asked you to decide what it would most likely eat. The correct answer is **Choice B**. Bugs are living creatures.

Using a Pictorial Format

When you read about something, you often build a picture in your mind. You read about Venus's-flytrap in Example 2. Maybe you tried to imagine what it looks like when this plant eats an insect.

Sometimes the ITBS Test will ask you to choose the picture that shows something you have read about.

Read the next example. It tells you how to cook something. Decide which picture shows what you are cooking.

❖ Example 3

Preheat oven to 375°.

Peel, core, and slice apples.

Arrange slices in an oven-proof dish.

Sprinkle with sugar, raisins, and bread crumbs.

Bake for 45 minutes.

3 **Which picture shows what you are cooking?**

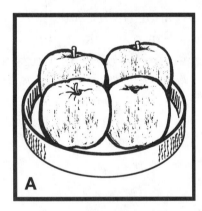
A

B

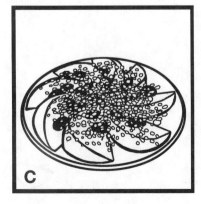
C

D

To answer this question correctly, you must read the recipe very carefully.

Choice A is wrong. It shows four baked apples. The selection told you to cut the apples into slices.

Choice B shows a loaf of bread. You had to use bread crumbs in this selection, but you didn't have to bake a loaf of bread.

Choice D shows a roast chicken. There was nothing about chickens in this selection.

Choice C shows a baked apple crisp. This is correct. The selection taught you how to prepare this dish.

Predicting Outcomes

When we predict an outcome, this is what we do: we use what we know about the past to guess what will happen in the future.

Predict the most likely outcome in the next example.

❖ Example 4

> Miranda got a bike for her birthday. At first she couldn't ride it. She kept falling down. But she kept trying, and now she rides everywhere.
>
> Then Miranda took some swimming lessons. At first she swam very badly.

4 **What do you think happened to Miranda later on?**
   A She gave up swimming.
   B She learned to swim well.
   C She began to hate the water.
   D She forgot how to ride a bike.

The best answer is **Choice B**. You read that Miranda couldn't ride her bike at first. But she kept trying and now she rides everywhere. You can predict that the same thing will happen with swimming. She will learn to swim well.

Helpful Hints
for MAKING GENERALIZATIONS
and APPLYING WHAT YOU HAVE LEARNED

1. Before you can make a generalization, you must first understand what happens in the passage.

2. To make a generalization, apply what happens to a broader situation or a wider group of people.

3. When you have to apply what you have learned, first decide what you concluded from the passage. Now check the new situation where you must apply this information. Find the answer choice that makes the most sense.

4. When you have to predict a story's outcome, ask yourself what is the story's main idea. Ask yourself how the characters in the story behave. Then decide which answer choice comes closest to what you think will happen next.

SELECTIONS FOR PRACTICE

✳ Selection 1

The Hawks are our high-school team. We like to watch them play. We cheer for them, and we are very happy when they win.

But recently, the Hawks have been playing poorly. They miss their shots. They even drop the ball. Their coach shouts at them all the time. It makes them nervous. The newspapers say a lot of Hawk players are getting sick.

1 **What will probably happen next time the Hawks play?**

A They will beat the other team.
B They will lose the game.
C They will miss the game.
D They will win the city championship.

* Selection 2

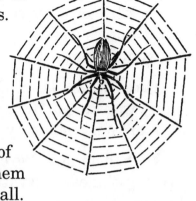

Anna-May hated spiders. She was afraid of them. She was also afraid of snakes and frogs. She never walked in the woods. She was too afraid of all the little animals.

Anna-May didn't want to be afraid. She went to college. She studied animals. She studied all the small animals she was afraid of. She even drew pictures of them for one of her classes. She had never really looked at them before. She decided they weren't so bad after all.

Now she is not afraid. She even likes spiders and frogs. She still doesn't like snakes, but she's not scared of them any more

2 **What can we learn from Anna-May's experience with spiders?**

A If you learn more about the things you're afraid of, they'll become less frightening.

B If you don't like bugs, you should avoid them.

C If you can draw a spider, you may become a fine artist.

D If you walk in the woods, you may see little animals that frighten you.

✽ Selection 3

Ella and Jack invited us to supper. They had just been married and were both learning to cook. The food tasted terrible. The fish was burned. The potatoes were not completely cooked. After the meal, we decided we would never eat at their house again.

Three weeks later, Ella and Jack invited us to supper again. We didn't want to go. But we didn't want to hurt their feelings. Ella and Jack are our friends, even if they are poor cooks.

We had an idea. We called and said we'd love to come and we'd like to bring Chinese food with us. They were a bit surprised, but they agreed. We bought the food at a take-out place, and everyone enjoyed the meal.

3 **How did the people telling the story feel when they ate the meal that Ella and Jack cooked?**

5 Describing and Analyzing Characters in Stories

Stories are usually about people. The people in a story are called the characters, and the author usually lets you know a lot about them. Sometimes they are brave. Sometimes they are funny. Or they may be weak, or lazy.

❖ **Example 1**

Ann went to the circus. She watched the lions. She bought popcorn and ate it all. She took pictures of everything she saw.

1 **Who is the most important character in the story?**

A   Ann
B   the circus
C   the popcorn
D   the pictures

The correct answer is **A, Ann**. A character is a person in the story. Ann is the only character in this story.

Some authors use words like brave or lazy or strong to describe their characters. Other authors make you figure out what their characters are like from what they do. Figure out how to describe Carlos.

❖ Example 2

> Carlos knew that bears were near. He couldn't see them, but he could hear them moving in the woods. He quickly built several fires around his tent. He kept the fires going all night. In the morning, the bears were gone.

2   How would you describe Carlos?

    A Lazy and poor
    B Old and weak
    C Smart and brave
    D Stupid

The correct choice is **C, smart and brave**. The author tells us that Carlos could hear the bears and that he built fires and kept them going all night. Carlos was very brave to do this and smart to figure out that fire would keep the bears away. All the other choices are wrong.

Comparing Characters

In some stories there are two or more characters. You may be asked to compare them. You do this by trying to decide how they are alike and how they are different.

❖ Example 3

> Hank just isn't interested in baseball. When his brother Fred watches baseball on TV, Hank reads a comic. Hank thinks football is exciting. He's happy to watch tennis. He likes every sport but baseball.

3   How are Hank and Fred different?

    A Fred prefers football, and Hank prefers baseball.
    B Fred likes sports, but Hank doesn't.
    C Hank likes sports, but Fred doesn't.
    D Hank prefers tennis to baseball.

The correct answer is **D, Hank prefers tennis to baseball**. You read that Hank reads a comic whenever Fred watches baseball on TV. Hank likes all sports except baseball. This tells you that the other choices are incorrect.

Helpful Hints
for Understanding the CHARACTERS in a Story

1. A character is a person in the story. Look for lines that tell you how the character acts.

2. Decide what word or words describe the character.

3. Sometimes there are two characters in the story. Decide how they are alike and how they are different.

SELECTIONS FOR PRACTICE

✳ Selection 1

Carl got married last Saturday. He married Alicia, whom he has known since kindergarten. Carl got lost on the way to the church. And he forgot the wedding ring. His sister Angie gave Carl her ring, and Carl used it for the ceremony. Later he found the missing ring. It was in his pocket all the time.

1 **How was Carl feeling on his wedding day?**

A Calm
B Nervous
C Sick
D Wonderful

NOTICE: Photocopying any part of this book is forbidden by law.

37

✳ Selection 2

> Dear Jan,
>
> Guess what? My aunt and uncle from Poland are coming to visit us! I've never met them. I wonder what they'll be like? They're going to bring my cousin with them. Her name is Marie, and she's just my age. My Dad says she likes American music. Do you think she'll like the same groups we do? You'll have to come over when she gets here!
>
> Nancy

2 **You can tell from the way Nancy writes to Jan that**

    A she's scared of her aunt and uncle.
    B she wants to go to Poland.
    C she likes her cousin a lot.
    D she is curious about her relatives.

✳ Selection 3

> Jesse was 6 foot 7 and tough as iron. But he had never been in the woods. His sister Chandra loved the woods. One Saturday, Jesse took a walk in the woods with Chandra. Jesse heard a lot of sounds. He heard one sound that seemed very close. Jesse looked worried. I guess he was afraid of snakes. But Chandra showed him where to look. She pointed down on the ground where a small bird was hopping in the leaves. Jesse laughed. Then he relaxed.

3 **How does Chandra differ from Jesse?**

    A She is bigger.
    B She is stronger.
    C She knows more about the woods.
    D She is better in reading and writing.

The Dog in the Manger
(*A fable by Aesop, a writer who lived in Ancient Greece*)

A Dog was looking for a place to take his afternoon nap. He saw a long box filled with straw that belonged to the Ox and jumped into it. He was lying there cozily upon the straw when the Ox returned from his afternoon work. The Ox came up to the box and wanted to eat some straw.

The Dog was furious at being awakened. He stood up and barked at the Ox whenever it tried to bite some straw.

At last the Ox gave up hope of getting at the straw and went away muttering: "Dog doesn't want to eat my straw. People often envy others having what they can't enjoy themselves."

4A **Which word best describes the Dog?**

A Easy-going
B Selfish
C Shy
D Unhappy

4B **At the end of the story, we see that the Ox is**

A gentle.
B kind.
C slow.
D fed up.

PART 3:
Evaluating Meaning

In Part Three of the ITBS Reading Coach you will see new kinds of questions about the meaning of a passage. You will think about the main idea of a selection and its theme. You will decide why the author wrote a selection. You will look at the way it is written. Then you will think about the author's style and how it helps you to understand and enjoy the passage.

6   Finding Main Ideas and Themes

The main idea tells what happened in the story.

Read the example below about dinosaurs. What is the main idea?

❖ Example 1

> Dinosaurs came in all shapes and sizes. Some were as big as a building. Others were as small as a chicken. Some walked on four legs. Others walked on two. Some were hunters who ate other animals. Some ate only plants.

1   **What is the main idea?**

   A   Dinosaurs ate other animals.
   B   Dinosaurs were very small.
   C   Some dinosaurs ate plants.
   D   There were many different kinds of dinosaurs.

The correct choice is **D, there were many different kinds of dinosaurs**. This is the most important idea. The selection also says that some dinosaurs were hunters, some ate plants, and some were very small. But these are just details. None of them is the most important idea of the selection.

Usually, the author doesn't tell you the main idea. You have to figure it out for yourself.

Now read about what underwater sounds are like. Figure out the main idea.

❖ Example 2

> Most people think that silence rules under the water. They think the bottom of the ocean is very quiet. But now we know they are wrong. Scientists have taken listening devices down to the bottom of the sea. They heard a lot of whistles, beeps, and grunts. One scientist said it sounded like a Chicago traffic jam with a lot of honking cars.

2 **The main idea is that**

    A poets are not very smart.
    B fish make beeps and whistles.
    C there is a lot of noise under the sea.
    D scientists study the ocean with listening devices.

The correct choice is **C, there is a lot of noise under the sea**. The author does not say this exactly. But if you read the selection, you can see that it is mainly about the noise under the sea.

There are many different ways to ask for the main idea of the story. Here are some of these ways.

- What is the topic of this story?
- What is this story about?
- What is the best title for the story?
- Which idea is most important?

Read Example 3. Answer a different kind of question about main ideas.

❖ Example 3

> In many old jungle films, gorillas were monsters. A movie gorilla was always super-strong and super-mean. But these ideas are not fair to real gorillas. Students of forest life paint a far different picture. Gorillas do not fight, except in self-defense. They do not eat meat when it is fed to them in zoos. Despite their powerful bodies and frightening appearance, they are quite peaceful.

3 **The best title for this selection is**

    A "Gorillas Are More Dangerous Than Lions."
    B "Gorillas Are Peaceful Animals."
    C "Gorillas Are Fierce Hunters."
    D "Gorillas Prefer Not to Eat Meat."

The correct choice is **B, "Gorillas Are Peaceful Animals."** This is what the selection is mostly about. It is the main idea. When a question asks for the best title, it is asking for the main idea.

Theme

A theme is something the story teaches you.

There are thousands of possible story themes. A story theme might be something like:

> Friends can keep secrets.

Or it might be:

> New clothes can make you feel good.

Usually the author doesn't tell you what the theme is. You have to figure it out.

❖ Example 4

> Tania got a big, beautiful doll for her birthday. It cost a lot of money. She also got great new blades to skate with. And she got three new CD's. But she still didn't feel happy.

4   **What is the theme of this story?**

    A Dolls cost too much.
    B CD's make good gifts.
    C Gifts alone don't make you happy.
    D Tania likes to skate.

The best answer is **C**. The gifts didn't make Tania happy. The selection shows that gifts alone don't make you happy. The selection doesn't say dolls cost too much or that CD's make good gifts. Choice D, Tania likes to skate, is not the theme of the selection. Tania might like to skate, but that is not what the selection teaches us about life.

Helpful Hints
for Finding MAIN IDEAS and THEMES

1. Imagine you have just read a story. Someone asks you, "What was the story about?" Ask yourself how you could sum up the story in one sentence. This will help you decide on the main idea of the story.

2. A story theme is something about life that the story teaches. Sometimes you have to figure it out from the story.

3. Don't pick a theme that sounds good but isn't in the story.

SELECTIONS FOR PRACTICE

✳ Selection 1

  I bought my car seven years ago. I haven't driven it for a year because I've been away. Yesterday I thought I'd get it ready to take it out on the road again. I had a real shock when I looked at it.

  The back window is cracked. Two of the lights won't go on. The motor needs a lot of work. The rear door won't open. I don't think I can afford to fix it. It's a shame. I liked my old car.

1 **The main idea is that**

  A new cars are expensive.
  B the car lights don't work.
  C the car is in very bad shape.
  D the writer has been away.

✳ Selection 2

> All the children love Mr. Zullo. He teaches them a lot and they have fun in his class. He brings in animals. He loves to read stories. He acts and talks like the people in the stories. He can talk like a king or a little girl or an old woman. He tells the children to draw pictures of the people in his stories. He makes the class laugh by playing jokes. He sings a song at the end of the day. He is special.

2 **What is the main idea of this story?**

    A Children like to play with snakes and puppies.
    B It's fun to have a story read to you.
    C Mr. Zullo is an extraordinary, wonderful teacher.
    D Mr. Zullo makes the children laugh all the time.

✳ Selection 3

> The little ballet dancer on top of the box was broken. One leg and arm had been chipped. But that didn't matter to Daisy. She thought it was the most beautiful music box she had ever seen. She touched the outside of the box. She put it next to her cheek. It felt very smooth. It was gold and black. The light made it shine in a pretty way. She opened it and the music started to play. It had a quiet, delicate sound. She smiled and started to dance.

3 **What is the theme of this story?**

    A How something looks matters more than anything.
    B It's fun to dance.
    C Music is more important than art.
    D You can love something that isn't perfect.

✳ Selection 4

It's very hard to earn a black belt in karate. A student must master hundreds of skills to reach this high level. The beginner practices constantly, aiming kicks and jabs at an imaginary partner. Later, the student learns a difficult series of moves called kata. Finally, the advanced student practices self-control. This last step is not easily learned. Some students never master it.

4A **The best title for this selection is**

A "Hundreds of Skills."
B "Learning Kata."
C "Practicing Kicks and Jabs."
D "Steps in Mastering Karate."

4B **According to the author, the most difficult task is**

A developing self-control.
B hardening the hand.
C jabbing at imaginary partners.
D wearing a belt.

7 Identifying the Author's Viewpoint and Purpose

If we study a passage, we can usually tell how the author feels about the people or things he or she describes. For example, see if you can figure out what the author thinks about her sister Luisa's bedroom in Example 1.

❖ Example 1

> My sister Luisa has her own bedroom. It has pale green walls, yellow curtains, and a purple rug. Whenever I go in there, I feel dizzy. The walls are covered with pictures of her favorite rock group—I can't think why she likes them! She likes the smell of lilacs, so she puts lilac perfume on her sheets and pillows. It smells so much I have to hold my nose.

1 The author seems to feel that

A Luisa's bedroom is quite pretty.
B she and Luisa like the same things.
C Luisa's room is awful.
D Luisa's room is too crowded.

The correct choice is **C, Luisa's room is awful**. You can tell this from the author's description. The colors make her dizzy. She hates the pictures of Luisa's favorite rock group. And she can't stand the strong smell of lilacs.

Read Example 2 and see if you can tell how the author feels about chimpanzees.

❖ Example 2

> Whenever I go to the zoo I like to spend a long time looking at the apes. Most of all, I like to watch the chimps. They are so cute! They spend a lot of time with each other. Then they like to swing from the branches in their cage. Their little faces remind me of people. Their eyes are so warm and soft. Sometimes they're a bit smelly, but I don't care. Also, I love to watch them eating bananas—they just love bananas.

2 **Which statement best shows the author's feeling about chimpanzees?**

- **A** They just love bananas.
- **B** They are so cute!
- **C** They smell bad sometimes.
- **D** They look like people.

The correct choice is **B**. The author says all the other things, too. But the statement that shows her feelings best is B. She likes watching chimps and thinks they're cute.

Authors have a general purpose in mind when they write. They may want to tell readers how to do something, or persuade readers to agree with them, or perhaps to make them laugh.

Read the next example and decide on its author's purpose.

❖ Example 3

How to Use the Morris Copier

Press the large ON button.

Press Regular Paper or Long Paper.

Set the number of copies you want.

Press the green START button.

---

3 **Why did the author write these lines?**

  A To amuse readers
  B To explain how to do something
  C To help people enjoy what they're reading
  D To get readers to agree

Choice B is correct. These lines are instructions on how to use a copying machine. Usually you'd find them in a manual. Instructions are easy to spot. They often have numbers in front of each step. And each step is a command; it tells you to do something.

Authors often have a particular purpose in writing.

Read the next example and decide what exactly the writer wanted to achieve.

❖ Example 4

The next time you put a battery in a toy, be careful. Look inside the place that holds the battery. You'll see a + sign at one end and a - sign at the other end. The battery also has a + sign at one end and a - sign at the other. Put the battery in so that its + end is at the + end of the place that holds it. The toy may not work if you don't do this.

---

4 **What did the author want readers to know?**

  A How to put a battery in a toy
  B Why some toys are dangerous
  C Why some toys need batteries
  D What + and - mean in math

Batteries have to be put into toys the right way. The author tells readers about this and warns them to make sure that the + end of the battery goes in the + end of the place that holds it. **Choice A** is correct.

Helpful Hints for
Understanding an AUTHOR'S POINT OF VIEW

1. As you read, see if the author uses words like "good" or "terrible" that show his or her point of view.

2. If not, think about the selection as you read. Ask yourself how the author felt about this topic.

3. The main reason authors write non-fiction passages is to teach their readers about something.

4. Where you read a selection may give you an important clue about why the author wrote it.

Read the next group of selections. Look at the words the author chooses. Then answer the questions about the author's point of view and purpose.

SELECTIONS FOR PRACTICE

❊ Selection 1

> The whole building was burning. But Ramon thought he heard a child's voice. Even though there was flame and smoke everywhere, Ramon kept looking for the child. The heat was terrible. Still, Ramon would not give up. He kept searching until he found the child and brought her safely out of the building.

1 **The author seems to feel that Ramon is**

  A brave.
  B cowardly.
  C lazy.
  D stupid.

❊ Selection 2

> I don't agree with people who say chess is a slow game. People who don't know much about chess think that players spend hours on a move. But they are wrong. Chess players move quite quickly. They usually take only a minute or two for a move.

2 **The author seems to feel that**

  A chess is actually a fairly fast game.
  B chess is only for old people.
  C chess is played very slowly.
  D only a genius can play chess.

✳ Selection 3

It was a tough game, tied three to three in the ninth. The Cubs manager walked up to the pitcher's mound. He and the pitcher talked. Then he pointed to the dugout and Wieszko came in to relieve.

3A **Who do you think the author wrote this passage for?**

   A Baseball fans
   B Historians
   C Scientists
   D Teachers

3B **Where might you find this type of selection?**

   A An atlas
   B A dictionary
   C A math book
   D A newspaper

> The F.B.I. regularly makes up a list of the nation's ten worst criminals. This list, called the "Ten Most Wanted," is posted as widely as possible. Pictures of the wanted men and women appear in post offices, newspapers, and police stations. Publicity helps the police to track down the people on the list. Once their faces become widely known, it is difficult for the criminals to hide.
>
> William Nesbit was on the first list the F.B.I. ever made up. He was involved in a jewel robbery. Afterwards, in another crime, he blew up a building using thousands of pounds of dynamite. The explosion was so strong it broke windows five miles away. Nesbit was caught when neighbors saw his picture in the paper and told police where he was hiding. Nesbit is only one of the many dozens of criminals who have been identified and captured because of the "Ten Most Wanted" list.

4A **The author seems to feel that**

    A Nesbit should have been given another chance.

    B the list didn't help to catch Nesbit.

    C the people on the list are not really bad.

    D the "Ten Most Wanted" list helps police find criminals.

4B **Why do you think the author writes about William Nesbit in the second paragraph?**

    A To describe the time he blew up a building and stole some jewels

    B To explain why neighbors told the police about Nesbit

    C To give an example of a criminal captured through the "Ten Most Wanted" list

    D To show that explosions can be strong enough to blow out windows

8 Interpreting Figurative Language

Writers and especially poets often use language in a special way, where the words don't mean exactly what they say. This is called figurative language or nonliteral language.

Read Example 1 and notice how the author describe the scene.

❖ Example 1

> The table groaned under all the dishes. Chickens, beef, ham, and all kinds of pies were piled high one upon the other. Ruby-red tomatoes and beets fought for space with grass-green lettuce and darker cucumbers. And in the corners shone the bright, glowing wine glasses and the narrow-necked bottles.

First, you may notice that the author never says what he is writing about. There is no need. You can tell that he is describing a great feast.

Now look at the actual words the author has used. He describes the table as groaning and the tomatoes as fighting for space with the lettuce. You know very well that tables don't groan and vegetables and fruits don't fight each other. But you can guess what this means. A groaning table is probably carrying a heavy weight. If things are fighting for space, they are crowded.

This unusual use of words gets our attention. It makes us take notice. Authors use figurative language to create vivid pictures for their readers.

Now reread the passage and answer the question.

1 **Why do you think the author describes the wine glasses as "bright" and "glowing"?**

   A They have light bulbs inside.
   B They have been polished until they shine.
   C They have cracks.
   D They are filled with soup.

The correct answer is **B**. Often you have to figure out what nonliteral language means by using your common sense. You can guess that the people who prepared this grand dinner wanted everything to look good. This includes the dishes and the glasses.

The other choices make no sense at all. Why put light bulbs into wine glasses if you want to drink out of them? Something with soup inside is not bright and glowing. And glasses with cracks don't glow.

Now try another example.

❖ Example 2

> Linda is only three years old but she swims like a fish. She is allowed to swim in the deep-water part of the pool because she swims so well. Now she's learning to dive.

2 **What does "Linda swims like a fish" mean?**

   A She is a very good swimmer.
   B She looks like a shark when she swims.
   C She stays under water for a long time.
   D She swims with her legs instead of her arms.

The correct answer is **A**. You learn that Linda swims very well. You know that fish swim very well. You can guess that swimming like a fish means swimming very well.

Helpful Hints for Understanding FIGURATIVE LANGUAGE

1. The term "figurative language" means using words and phrases in an unusual way where they don't mean exactly what they say.

2. Authors use figurative language to give their writing more color and power.

3. You can often use context clues to understand what the author means.

✳ Selection 1

> Some trees are built broad and close to the ground, like a wrestler. Some trees stand straight and pencil-thin. Some trees bear clouds of flowers, while others never bloom. Some tree trunks are as gray as a stormy sky and others are pale green.

1 **What point is the author trying to make when she compares trees to pencils, wrestlers, clouds, and stormy skies?**

    A   Children love to climb trees and build tree houses.
    B   Trees come in many different sizes and colors.
    C   The most beautiful trees have flowers.
    D   Some trees change like the weather.

✳ Selection 2

> **At Sea**
>
> Leaning and turning,
> The white sails move
> Soft with the breeze
> In a slow, gentle waltz.
> Shadows of danger
> Break through the waves.
> With sharp, pointed claws,
> The rocks wait for their prey.
> Calmly, the sailor
> Pulls at the rudder.
> The rocks grow smaller,
> Cheated of their prize.

2A **The poet describes the rocks' "sharp, pointed claws" to show that**

    A   the boat's white sails have been torn by the wind.
    B   the fierce wind was howling like a beast.
    C   the rocks' rough edges could destroy a boat.
    D   the waves fear the rocks.

2B **This poem is about**

    A   danger and safety.

    B   the beauty of the sea.

    C   the joy of sailing

    D   the gentle lapping of the waves.

2C **Why does the poet write that the "rocks grow smaller"?**

    A   The sailor is looking for new rocks that are smaller than the earlier rocks.

    B   The sailor has passed the rocks and they look smaller now that they are further away.

    C   The sailor cannot see the rocks because of the sea spray.

    D   The rising tide is covering the rocks and making them look tiny.

✳ Selection 3

Cheryl awoke with a start. The storm was shaking the windows so fiercely she thought they would shatter.

It had been raining when she went to sleep, but nothing like this. Cheryl lay shaking in bed; her heart felt like a jet plane taking off. She closed her eyes and tried to relax.

Then came a mighty clap of thunder. Cheryl saw a bolt of lightning flash outside her bedroom window. Quickly, she leaped from her bed and grabbed her robe.

3 **In the second paragraph, what does it mean to say that Cheryl's "heart was a jet plane taking off"?**

    A   Her heart felt as though it had stopped beating.

    B   Her heart was beating very fast.

    C   She felt like laughing and crying at the same time.

    D   She couldn't hear herself think.

PART 4:
Practice Tests

• •

The last part of this book has two Practice Tests. The first one is followed by a discussion of the answers. Don't peek at the answers until you have finished the test and your teacher lets you do so.

When you get to the second test, you will be on your own.

Do the best you can on these Practice Tests. They will help you get ready for the ITBS.

Before you begin Practice Test 1, read the Test-Taking Tips on the following pages.

Test-Taking Tips

First tip: Relax. Take it easy.

This book has prepared you for all of the types of questions that appear on the ITBS Reading Test.

Don't get stuck on any question. Make the best decision you can. Answer the question, even if you are not sure of the answer.

Then go on.

Relax.

Follow the tips on the next two pages.

Pay Attention to Questions

It is important to read questions carefully. Some questions may ask you to decide what is TRUE. Other questions may ask you to decide what is NOT TRUE.

Read and answer Example 1.

❖ Example 1

1   **Which person was NOT a President of the United States?**

   A   Abraham Lincoln
   B   Muhammad Ali
   C   Bill Clinton
   D   George Washington

Think-Along

If you paid attention to the word NOT, you know the answer is **B, Muhammad Ali**.

Eliminate Wrong Answers

In some cases, you may not be sure of an answer. You may know two of the answer choices are wrong. Eliminate the wrong answers and make the best guess you can. Then go on. Try this on the next question.

❖ Example 2

2   **Which person was an American writer?**

    A   Adolph Hitler
    B   Christopher Columbus
    C   Queen Elizabeth
    D   Pearl Buck

Think-Along

The correct answer is **D, Pearl Buck**. You probably didn't know that Pearl Buck was a writer. But you could figure it out. You probably know that Columbus is a wrong answer and that Queen Elizabeth is also wrong. You can eliminate these two choices. Maybe you also know that Hitler was a German dictator. Only Pearl Buck is left. So Pearl Buck must be the writer.

Practice Test 1 With Feedback

Now you are ready to start the first practice test. After you finish it, your teacher will go over the answers with you.

This passage tells about a ride that Kaiisa took. Can you figure out what is happening in the story?

❖ Example 1

> Kaiisa closed her eyes. The car dived downwards. Kaiisa held on tight to her seat. All around her, people screamed happily. Suddenly the car zoomed upwards. It slowed, and then plunged down again.

1 **Where is Kaiisa?**

   A Having a birthday party
   B On a roller-coaster
   C Taking an exam in school
   D Watching a movie

The correct answer is **B, on a roller-coaster**. The selection tells about a car that dived down, zoomed up, and then dived down again. It contained people screaming happily. You can guess that the car was part of a roller-coaster ride.

Directions: First read the paragraph. Then read the questions. Pick the best answer to each question.

May 1, 1996

Dear Jason,

Thanks for the sweater you sent me for my birthday. I was happy you picked blue. I always look my best in blue or light green.

I had a great birthday. We are going to have a big Thanksgiving party this year. I hope you will be here then.

Love,

Sue-Ann

---

1 **Why did Sue-Ann write this letter?**

A To send Jason a small present
B To tell Jason about her birthday party
C To thank Jason for his gift
D To wish Jason a happy birthday

2 **What did Sue-Ann seem to like best about the gift?**

J She liked the color.
K She said it would be good for Thanksgiving.
L She said she didn't have any other sweaters.
M She thought the sweater would be warm.

3 **Why does Sue-Ann tell Jason about the Thanksgiving party?**

A She wants Jason to feel jealous.
B She wants Jason to come to the party.
C She wants Jason to send her a gift.
D She wants to show Jason her sweater.

The feats of the world's strongest men and women are almost beyond belief. Rama Murtu Naidu, called "The Indian Hercules," once supported the weight of a 7,000-pound elephant. An ordinary person would be crushed by so heavy a weight. Josephine Blatt once lifted 3,456 pounds. She did this lift in front of a large theater audience, so we can be sure it really happened. Louis Cyr lifted a platform on which 18 men were sitting—a lift of well over 4,000 pounds. He also lifted a 535-pound. weight off the floor using a single finger. Siegmund Breitbent bit his way through a steel bar!

But the most incredible stunt of all was carried out by Frank Richards. He stood next to a cannon which fired a cannon ball into his stomach. His stomach was so strong that the cannon ball bounced back. These feats may seem impossible, but we are sure they actually happened.

4 **What is the best title for this selection?**

J "Cannon Ball Belly"
K "How to Lift an Elephant"
L "Proof Exists"
M "Strong Men and Women"

5 **Who saw Josephine Blatt's famous lift?**

A A large theater audience
B Cannonball Richards
C Nobody
D Siegmund Breitbent

6 **What did "The Indian Hercules" do?**

J He let an elephant stand on him.
K He lifted 3,456 pounds.
L He picked up a platform with 18 men on it.
M He stood in the way of a cannonball.

7 · **The author seems to feel that**

A   nobody knows if these stories are true.

B   the weight lifters of today could do better than the people described in the story.

C   these stunts really were done.

D   it is easy to understand how to lift such weights if you know a few tricks.

It was a summer day. Mr. Crow was hot and wanted a drink. He started to dive into the farmer's well, but it had dried up in the sun. So then he tried to take a sip from the lake, but it had dried up, too. He was very upset. "At this rate, I'll never get anything to drink," he said to himself.

Then Mr. Crow spied a pitcher next to the farmer's barn. He went over to see what was inside it. There was some water left in the pitcher.

"But how can I get it out?" he asked. "If I tip over the pitcher, the water will spill out. If I try to put my bill into the pitcher, I could slip and tumble into it."

Mr. Crow was very sad. "I could drink that water if I could just think of a way to get it," he said.

Just then Mr. Crow spotted a pile of pebbles. "I've got it!" he cried.

Mr. Crow went over to the pile of pebbles. He picked up a black pebble with his bill. He went to the pitcher of water and dropped the pebble in. Then he went back to the pile and picked up a brown pebble. And he dropped that one into the pitcher. He went to the pile and back to the pitcher six times. Then he rested. After that, he made nine trips and rested again. At last, after lots and lots of trips, he was done.

Mr. Crow smiled. He put his bill into the pitcher and drank and drank. Then he flew up into a tree to rest.

He said to himself, "A little at a time does the trick!"

8 **What tells you that the character in this story is not a person?**

J   The character doesn't know how to think.
K   The character picks up things with his beak and is named Mr. Crow.
L   The character does not have real feelings.
M   The character is too stupid to be real.

9 **Why was Mr. Crow happy by the end of this story?**

A   He got what he wanted without doing anything.
B   He met a lovely lady crow.
C   He was safe in a tree.
D   He was no longer thirsty.

10 **Why did Mr. Black Crow fill the pitcher with pebbles?**

J   To hide them so he could use them later on
K   To prevent other crows from finding out about the water
L   To raise the height of the water until he could reach it
M   To weigh it down so it wouldn't tip over

11 **Which line from the story sums up its theme?**

A   "A little at a time does the trick!"
B   After lots and lots of trips, his job was finished.
C   "At this rate, I'll never get anything to drink."
D   "I have it!" he cried.

12 **What do you learn about Mr. Black Crow?**

J   He gives up easily.
K   He has a lot of imagination.
L   He is lazy.
M   He is very frightened.

Section 1

Today, Florida is famous for its oranges. One hundred years ago, Florida didn't grow many oranges. The problem was the weather. Most of the time, even in winter, Florida has warm weather. But sometimes freezing weather comes from the north. In the past, when these cold snaps came, the oranges died.

Today, Florida has a different kind of orange that can live through cold weather. This is the story of how Florida got this orange. It is the story of a Chinese American called Lue Gim Gong. With Lue's help, Florida became the land of oranges.

Section 2

Lue was born in China. He was only 12 years old when he sailed to America. He went to live in Massachusetts where a Sunday-school teacher named Fanny Burlingame taught him to speak English.

Fanny loved plants. She had a large garden and Lue helped in her greenhouses. He was only a teenager, but he knew a lot about working with plants. Back home in China, his mother had taught him many tricks. He knew how to graft plants. This meant he could take one type of plant and join it onto another. The new plant was like both plants, then.

Lue liked working for Fanny, but he had to stop. He became ill with a lung disease called tuberculosis. He went back home to China. To everyone's surprise, Lue recovered.

Section 3

One day, he had a letter from Fanny. She had bought land in Florida and was trying to grow oranges. However, the oranges weren't doing well. They were ruined by heavy rain or cold weather. Fanny wanted Lue to save her oranges. So Lue returned to America.

Lue decided to create a stronger orange. He used his skill in grafting. He grafted a Florida orange onto an orange from southern Europe. The new orange was a sweet, juicy fruit. Most important, it could stand the cold. It was named the Lue Gim Gong orange. In 1911, Lue's orange was awarded a medal.

Soon after this, Fanny Burlingame died. In her will, she left all her Florida land to Lue. Lue continued to grow his new kind of oranges. He also created a new kind of grapefruit. He created new currants and peaches, too. Lue Gim Gong was a genius with plants.

13 **When did Lue Gim Gong go to Florida?**

   A After he left China for the first time
   B After he recovered from tuberculosis
   C After he made a new kind of orange
   D Before he went to Massachusetts

14 **What made Lue Gim Gong so helpful to Fanny Burlingame?**

   J He was good at giving things new names.
   K He knew a lot about lung diseases.
   L He knew a lot about plants.
   M He wanted to live in the United States.

15 **What is one way to create a new kind of plant?**

   A Graft one kind of plant onto another
   B Cut a plant stem in half and stick it in the ground
   C Use only plants from Florida
   D Grow plants in heavy rain or cold weather

16 **What kind of weather change would have made Lue Gim Gong's work unnecessary?**

   J If it rained more in Florida
   K If Florida never had cold weather
   L If it didn't get so hot in Florida in the summer months
   M If there were no hurricanes in Florida

17 **Why did Lue Gim Gong return to China?**

   A He was very sick with tuberculosis.
   B He needed to learn more about plants from his mother.
   C Fanny Burlingame had left Massachusetts.
   D He wasn't allowed to stay in the United States any more.

Brothers
by Sophie Jenkins

All day long
They sleep now,
Curled around
Each other.

Bad gums, bad teeth
Sleeping, eating
Lazy cats, old cats
All day they sleep.

Something slides by the corner.
They jump up, ears twitching,
Alert now and waiting,
All ready to pounce.

18 What made the cats wake up in the third verse of this poem?

J It was their dinner time.
K They had a tooth ache.
L They saw a mouse.
M They had been sleeping all day and they wanted to stretch.

19 The cats

A are very beautiful
B fight all the time.
C like to hunt in the woods.
D sleep a lot.

20 What kind of contrast does the poet make between the first two verses and the last verse?

J Between being hungry and being satisfied
K Between being old and being young
L Between being sick and being well
M Between being sleepy and being wide awake

21 **What does the title of the poem tell you about these two cats?**

   A They had the same parents.
   B They prefer to be outdoors.
   C They are very old for cats.
   D They are fierce hunters.

Section 1

The Aztec Indians lived in Mexico hundreds of years ago. Their main city was built on islands in a lake. It was a crowded place. Thousands of people lived there, and they all had to be fed. Every inch of soil was used to grow food. But the farmers needed still more soil. They found it in an odd place. They scraped it from the bottom of the lake. This soil was placed on floating rafts made of reeds and roots. The farmers then grew food on their rafts.

Section 2

The Aztecs were skilled farmers. Some of our favorite foods were first grown by them. Chocolate and cocoa are Aztec foods. The Aztecs also grew corn, wild bananas, tomatoes, avocados, and beans. One of their most important crops was a plant with large, thick, spiny leaves. It was called the maguey (pronounced mah-GAY).

Section 3

Aztecs found many uses for the maguey. They drank juice pressed from its leaves. They ate its roots. They wrote on a kind of paper made from it. Aztec scribes recorded laws, legends and rituals on this paper. Thread, rope, and cloth sandals came from maguey fibers. The maguey has sharp thorns. The Aztecs made pins and needles from them. The leaves were used in the walls and roofs of their houses.

22 In Section 3, you read about the Aztec scribes. What are "scribes"?

J Builders
K Rulers
L Painters
M Writers

23 What is the main thing you learn in Section 1?

A How the Aztecs grew their food
B Where the Aztecs lived
C Why the Aztecs used boats to catch fish
D What kind of food the Aztecs ate

24 What was the author's purpose in writing the last paragraph?

J To describe the many uses of the maguey
K To explain why the Aztecs needed fibers
L To stress how hard life was for the Aztecs
M To warn readers about the maguey's sharp thorns

25 Where would you be most likely to read a passage like this?

A In a newspaper
B In an encyclopedia
C In a book about farming in the Midwest
D In a fashion magazine

26 What did an Aztec farmer look like?

This is the story of a doctor who helped many animals.

Section 1

Dr. Doolittle was an animal doctor. He was the only doctor who could talk to animals, and he saved the life of thousands of them. But Dr. Doolittle was poor. That's because animals have no money, and so they couldn't pay him.

The animals were unhappy because Dr. Doolittle had no money to buy food or clothes. They decided to help him. They held a big meeting and came up with a plan to help the doctor. They would bring him a very rare animal called the pushmi-pullyu. This animal had two heads. Dr. Doolittle could take the pushmi-pullyu to a circus. Then he could get rich.

Section 2

Pushmi-pullyus are now extinct. But long ago, when Doctor Doolittle was alive, there were still some left. There were very few and they lived in the deepest jungles. Pushmi-pullyus had no tail, but a head at each end. They were very shy and terribly hard to catch. You couldn't sneak up on them, because they could look both ways. And you couldn't catch them while they were sleeping, because only one head was asleep. The other head was always awake and watching.

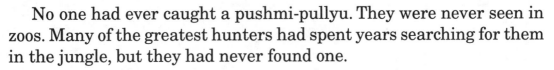

No one had ever caught a pushmi-pullyu. They were never seen in zoos. Many of the greatest hunters had spent years searching for them in the jungle, but they had never found one.

Only the animals knew where to find a pushmi-pullyu, and it was even hard for them. But after a long time hunting, they found one.

NOTICE: Photocopying any part of this book is forbidden by law.

73

Section 3

The animals asked the pushmi-pullyu if he would go with Dr. Doolittle. He would be in a circus for a year.

But he shook both his heads and said, "Certainly not!"

They explained he wouldn't be shut up in a cage. People would just look at him. They said Dr. Doolittle was kind and poor. People would pay a lot of money to see a pushmi-pullyu. Then Dr. Doolittle would get rich and he could keep taking care of the animals.

But the pushmi-pullyu shook his heads. "No, I won't go. You know how shy I am. I hate being stared at." And he almost began to cry.

But the animals kept talking to him. They said Dr. Doolittle would take care of him. They said he could come back home to the jungle in a year. And they said that all the animals should help Dr. Doolittle because he had cured so many sick animals.

After a while the pushmi-pullyu said he would talk to Dr. Doolittle. He talked for a whole day. Then he said he would go to the circus with Dr. Doolittle.

27 **What is the best summary of this story?**

  A Dr. Doolittle was an animal doctor.
  B The animals wanted to help Dr. Doolittle because he had helped them.
  C The pushmi-pullyu is a rare animal with two heads and no tail.
  D Dr. Doolittle found a way of making the animals rich.

28 **Why would people pay a lot of money to see a pushmi-pullyu?**

  J He lived in a jungle.
  K He had two heads.
  L He was both fish and animal.
  M He was so fat.

29 **In Section Two, what does "extinct" mean?**

  A Not existing any more
  B Very expensive
  C Shy
  D Having two heads

30 **How did the pushmi-pullyu feel about being in a circus?**

  J He didn't like to be stared at.
  K He liked the crowds.
  L He hoped he would be a clown and make children laugh.
  M He wanted to get rich.

31 **What probably happened after a year's time?**

  A Dr. Doolittle stopped helping animals.
  B The animals found another animal doctor.
  C The pushmi-pullyu went back to the jungle.
  D The pushmi-pullyu became a doctor.

32 **Where does most of this story take place?**

  J In a circus
  K In a jungle
  L In a zoo
  M In a park

Feedback

1. **Choice C** is correct. Sue-Ann wanted to thank Jason for his gift. The letter had other things in it, but its main purpose was to thank Jason.

2. **She liked the color, Choice J**, is the correct answer. Sue-Ann didn't say that the sweater would be good for Thanksgiving or that it would be warm, or that she didn't have any other sweaters. She did say that she was happy Jason picked the color blue.

3. The correct answer is **B, she wants Jason to come to the party**.

4. **Choice M** is the best answer. This selection tells you about four strong men and one strong women.

5. The passage tells you that an audience saw Josephine Blatt lift 3,456 pounds. **Choice A** is correct.

6. **Choice J** is correct. "The Indian Hercules" once let an elephant stand on him.

7. The correct answer is **Choice C**. The author writes that these feats may seem impossible, but we are sure they happened. This tells you that the author believes these stories to be true.

8. **Choice K** is correct. Crows, but not people, pick things up in their beaks. The other choices are not correct. We know from the story that Mr. Crow is very smart, and that he has real feelings—he's upset when he thinks he won't be able to quench his thirst. He is pleased with himself when he solves this problem.

9. **Choice D** is correct. Mr. Crow has worked out a way to reach the water and drink it. He is no longer thirsty.

10. **Choice L** is the right answer. Each time he dropped a pebble into the pitcher, the water rose a little higher. After he put enough pebbles in, he could drink the water.

11. Mr. Crow says, "A little at a time does the trick," because he raised the water little by little, pebble by pebble. **Choice A** is correct.

12. Everything you learn about Mr. Crow tells you that he has lots of imagination. He imagined how he might solve his problem. **Choice K** is correct.

13. This question asks you to find the order in which things happened. Lue Gim Gong went from China to Massachusetts. Then he became sick and returned to China. While he was there, he had a letter from Fanny Burlingame asking him to go to Florida. **Choice B** is correct.

14. **Choice L** is correct. Fanny Burlingame grew plants and, later on, fruit. Lue Gim Gong was useful to her because he knew so much about plants.

15. **Choice A** is correct. In Section Two, you learn all about making new plants by grafting a piece of one plant onto another plant.

16. Lue Gim Gong created a new orange that could handle cold weather. If there was no cold weather in Florida, there would be no need for this kind of orange. **Choice K** is correct.

17. **Choice A** is correct. You read in the story that Lue Gim Gong became very sick with tuberculosis and had to return to China.

18. The cats saw a mouse. **Choice L** is correct.

19. You read at the start of the poem that the cats sleep all day. **Choice D** is correct.

20. In the first two verses of the poem, the cats are sleeping. In the final verse, they are wide awake. **Choice M** is correct.

21. The title tells you that the cats in the poem are brothers. This means that they had the same parents. **Choice A** is correct.

22. "Scribes" are writers. **Choice M** is correct.

23. This section tells you all about how the Aztecs grew their food. **Choice A** is correct.

24. The last paragraph tells you the many ways that the Aztecs used the maguey plant. **Choice J** is correct.

25. You would be most likely to read a passage like this in an encyclopedia. **Choice B** is correct. Encyclopedias have lots of information about history and science. Newspapers mostly carry today's news, so Choice A is incorrect. The Aztecs lived in Mexico, not in the Midwest, so Choice C is incorrect. Choice D makes no sense.

26. You read in Section 1 about how the Aztecs grew their food. You read about the boats that were used as farms. You also read about the farmers who moved these boats around with their poles. The picture in **Choice M** shows what an Aztec farmer looked like.

27. The correct choice is **B, the animals wanted to help Dr. Doolittle because he had helped them**. Choice A and Choice C are details from the story. Choice D is not correct.

28. The correct choice is **K, he had two heads**. People like to look at strange, unusual creatures.

29. Something that is "extinct" doesn't exist anymore. **Choice A** is correct. You can guess this when you read in the story, "But long ago, when Dr. Doolittle was alive, there were still some left."

30. **Choice J, he didn't like to be stared at**, is the correct answer. The pushmi-pullyu says this in the story.

31. The correct choice is **C, the pushmi-pullyu went back to the jungle**. You can't be sure of this but the animals said this is what would happen.

32. The correct choice is **K, in a jungle**.

18 Practice Test 2

❖ Example 1

This passage tells about Sonia, who likes to cook.

> Sonia liked to cook. She always sang while she cooked. Sometimes her sister Anita helped Sonia prepare dinner. Sonia joked with Anita and made her laugh. Sonia was the kind of person people like to be around.

1 **Sonia is**

    A   a lot of fun.

    B   efficient.

    C   shy.

    D   smart.

Directions: First read the paragraph. Then read the question. Pick the best answer.

The correct answer is **A, a lot of fun**. Sonia sang while she cooked. She made her sister laugh. People liked to be around her. You can guess that she's a lot of fun.

Read this passage. Can you guess how Jaime feels at the end of the day?

❖ **Example 2**

> Jaime has a new job. He works very hard. He lifts heavy boxes all day. At the end of the day, he has to have a nap before his supper.

2   How would you describe Jaime at the end of the day?

   A Calm
   B Strong
   C Tired
   D Worried

The correct answer is **C, tired**. Jaime works very hard and he needs to take a nap when he gets home.

The Sides of the Sea
by Michelle Matthews

I can smell it now,
Salty, sharp, and sweet,
The smell of the sea.
I can hear them now,
Muffled and thumping,
The sound of the waves.
I can see it now,
Darker blue below
(Lighter blue above)
I see where they join.
Now I can see
Where the sky meets the sea.

1 **This poem is called "The Sides of the Sea." What does this title refer to?**

A How some people like the sea more than others do
B Different ways of thinking about the sea
C The fact that the sea has high and low tides
D The ocean beaches that face the sea

2 **Why does the poet describe the waves as "Muffled and thumping"?**

J To tell the reader how they sounded to her
K To tell the reader what they looked like
L To tell the reader what they reminded her of
M To tell the reader what the weather was like

3 **In the poem, you read about the "lighter blue above." What is the poet describing in this line?**

A The clouds
B The sea
C The sky
D The waves

NOTICE: Photocopying any part of this book is forbidden by law.

81

Mr. Mash invented things. He could make toys, tools, cars, and much more. Everyone liked Mr. Mash. He always smiled. He wore round wire glasses when he did his job. But Mr. Mash had one bad habit. He was forgetful.

One day Brad, the baker, came in to see Mr. Mash. "Can you help me?" Brad said. "It takes me too long to twist pretzels by hand. Can you invent a pretzel twister for me?"

Mr. Mash nodded. "Come back in two days. Your pretzel twister will be waiting," he said.

Just then the shop bell rang. Margo Malone, the policewoman, dashed in. She was very angry.

"The streets are so jammed with cars and trucks that I can't get anywhere," Margo said. "What I need is a motorcycle that flies. Then I can fly over the streets and do my job better. Can you invent one for me?"

Mr. Mash smiled. "Come back in two days, and I'll have one for you," he said.

After Margo left, a little girl named Kathy came in with her toy puppet. "Mr. Mash," she said, "can you invent a way to make my puppet sing? I want to pull one of its strings and make it sing happy songs."

Mr. Mash asked Kathy to come back in two days. He said he would have a singing puppet for her then.

When Kathy left, Mr. Mash put on his glasses. He made plans for the pretzel twister, the flying motorcycle, and the singing puppet. Mr. Mash was fast, and he quickly drew three plans.

The next day Mr. Mash went back to his shop. He forgot where he had left his glasses. He looked and looked but could not find them anywhere. He tried to read the plans he had devised, but he could not see them without his glasses.

"Oh, well," he said to himself, "I can get along without my plans. I never forget the plans I make."

So Mr. Mash started to put together the three things he had invented. Soon everything was finished. Mr. Mash sent for Brad, Margo, and Kathy.

Margo took her motorcycle outside and started it up. Brad pushed a button on the pretzel twister. Kathy pulled a string to make her puppet sing.

Then what do you think happened?

Margo's motorcycle did not fly. It started to play a loud song. Brad's pretzel twister did not make anything. It started to fly around the shop. Kathy's puppet did not sing a note. But out of its lips popped a twisted pretzel.

Mr. Mash just looked and scratched his chin. "What did I do?" he said. "Without my glasses, I got the plans mixed up!"

Then Brad smiled. He said, "I think the next thing you should invent is a way not to forget things."

4　**From the author's description of Mr. Mash, you would expect that**

   J　he has a lot of friends.

   K　he has trouble finding work.

   L　he is rather lonely.

   M　he eats too much.

5　**Why did Margo need a flying motorcycle?**

   A　So she could go shopping

   B　So she could get around more quickly

   C　So she could leave the police station without anyone seeing her

   D　So she could take care of lost planes

6　**This story is mostly about how Mr. Mash**

   J　invents new toys for Christmas.

   K　makes things for children.

   L　loses his eyeglasses.

   M　gets mixed up and makes the wrong things.

7　**Why didn't Mr. Mash use his plans to build Kathy's singing puppet?**

   A　He never worked from plans.

   B　He decided that Kathy really wanted a puppet that made pretzels instead.

   C　He lost his glasses and couldn't find them.

   D　He was a very slow worker.

8 **How would you guess Brad feels about Mr. Mash's mistakes?**

J   He is angry.
K   He doesn't care.
L   He thinks it's funny.
M   He is scared.

9 **You read about the plans Mr. Mash devised. What would you guess "devised" means?**

A   Destroyed
B   Created
C   Borrowed
D   Forgot

Many people say that Leroy Paige, or "Satchel" Paige, as he was called, was the best pitcher in baseball history. He grew up at a time when black players were not allowed in the Major Leagues. Most of his career was spent pitching for black baseball teams, where he was a great star.

Late in his career, the Major Leagues finally began to allow black players to play on their teams. Satchel Paige was one of the first black pitchers to be signed, entering the Majors at an age when most players have already retired. He continued to pitch in the Majors for many years. He was still good enough to be brought back to pitch when he reached the age of 59, which made him the oldest pitcher in baseball history. If he had joined the Major Leagues at the usual age of 19 or 20, he might have broken all the records in Major League pitching history.

10 **How good does the author seem to think Paige was when he pitched for a black baseball team?**

J   Almost ready for the Majors
K   Better than any other pitcher, black or white
L   Just learning his trade
M   An average pitcher

11 **You read that Satchel Paige began pitching for the Major Leagues late in his career. Why was this?**

A He was better at hitting than at pitching.
B Black players could not play in the Major Leagues for many years.
C It took many years before he became a really fine baseball player.
D The Major Leagues liked younger players better.

12 **Why might "The Tragedy of Satchel Paige" be a good title for this selection?**

J His life was filled with sadness and loss.
K He had to stop playing because of injuries.
L Most baseball fans didn't see him when he was at his peak.
M No one ever knew what a great baseball talent he was.

Section 1

Virginia loves all music. But what she likes best is the guitar. She spends an hour every day after school practicing. And she spends all day Saturday playing, too.

Section 2

She thinks about music all the time. Sometimes you can see her in the lunchroom. Everyone else is talking. She just hums. She doesn't have a guitar in school. But she moves her fingers all during class like she's practicing. Her teacher doesn't mind. He just smiles at Virginia.

Section 3

When Virginia picks up her guitar, her classmates listen to her with rapt attention. She's only 11, but she's going to play at the school dance. Everyone else in the band is at least 16. She's as good as anyone in the band.

Section 4

Both of Virginia's brothers play music. Paul plays the drums. Omar plays the trumpet. They are both older than Virginia. But neither of them was invited to play in the band. They don't play as well as Virginia. Paul and Omar don't like to practice. Virginia practices a lot.

13 **What is the main idea in this story?**

   A Paul plays in the band.
   B Omar doesn't practice much.
   C Virginia hums in class instead of talking.
   D Virginia plays the guitar well and plays in the band.

14 **The author seems to feel that**

   J it is very hard to play the guitar well.
   K Paul and Omar will get better in the years to come.
   L the school band plays good rock music.
   M Virginia is good because she practices.

15 **What will probably happen when Virginia plays at the school dance?**

   A She'll be too nervous to play.
   B Omar will play the trumpet.
   C The crowds will love listening to her.
   D Virginia will forget her guitar.

16 **In Section Three you read that Virginia's classmates listen to her with "rapt attention." This means that**

   J they don't understand her music very well.
   K they listen very, very carefully.
   L they make a lot of noise when she plays.
   M they clap their hands to show they like her music.

Section 1

Poison ivy is a plant. It grows in many parts of the country. It spreads along the ground. It climbs trees and fences. It grows everywhere.

Section 2

People who brush against poison ivy get a rash. Their skin itches, and it makes them want to scratch. Poison ivy won't kill you, but it makes you feel very unhappy.

A very few people are lucky. They are immune to poison ivy. They never get a rash. Others need to see a doctor or even go to the hospital.

People often get poison ivy when they walk in the woods. Long sleeves and long pants will help protect your arms and legs. But it is still easy to get a rash on the fingers or hands.

Section 3

The best way to recognize poison ivy is by its leaves. They are always found in groups of three. Be careful with any plant with three leaves! In the summer the leaves are a dark, shiny green. They are really quite pretty. But in the fall the color changes. The leaves turn to red or brown.

Don't touch poison ivy. The plant has an oil that gets on your skin and causes the rash. If you touch poison ivy, wash the oil off. Wash as soon as possible with strong soap and water. You must wash for a long time. You can't see the oil, but it sticks to your skin and is hard to wash off.

17 **A good title for this selection is**

   A "Plants to Avoid."
   B "Poison Ivy Leaves Are Pretty."
   C "Walking in the Woods."
   D "Watch Out for Poison Ivy."

18 **Poison ivy leaves are**

   J always green.
   K found in groups of three.
   L hard to find.
   M spiny.

19 **What should you do if you touch poison ivy?**

   A Put cream on your skin
   B See a doctor
   C Wash your skin
   D Wear gloves

20 **Why do you think the author describes poison ivy so carefully in Section Three?**

   J Because it is such a pretty plant
   K Because she wants readers to know what it looks like so they can avoid it
   L Because she wants readers to compare her description with the picture of poison ivy
   M Because she is writing this passage for scientists

21 **Poison oak is a poisonous ground plant like poison ivy. It also has three leaves that turn red in the fall. What conclusion might you draw from this?**

   A Fall colors include red, orange, brown, and gold.
   B Red leaves are more beautiful than leaves of any other color.
   C When a plant's leaves turn red, fall has arrived.
   D In the fall, you shouldn't touch ground plants with three red leaves.

22 **In Section 2 of this passage, "immune" means**

  J cured.
  K not harmed by.
  L poisoned.
  M unknown.

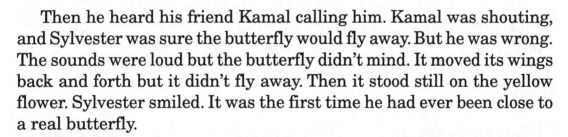

Sylvester lived in a big city. He liked looking at pictures of butterflies in books. But he had never been close to a real butterfly.

Today Mrs. Patrick took the whole class to the park. Everyone but Sylvester was by the lake. Sylvester was all alone. He saw something float on the air. A big colorful butterfly landed on a flower. The butterfly— all orange and black—was still. Sylvester stood there looking. His books said it was easy to scare a butterfly. So Sylvester didn't move.

Then he heard his friend Kamal calling him. Kamal was shouting, and Sylvester was sure the butterfly would fly away. But he was wrong. The sounds were loud but the butterfly didn't mind. It moved its wings back and forth but it didn't fly away. Then it stood still on the yellow flower. Sylvester smiled. It was the first time he had ever been close to a real butterfly.

23 **Why didn't Sylvester make a sound?**

  A He was too surprised to speak.
  B He didn't want to scare the butterfly.
  C He was tired and wanted to sleep.
  D He didn't want to bother Mrs. Patrick.

24 How did Sylvester feel about the butterfly?

J He didn't want anyone else to see it.
K He hoped it would fly away.
L He liked looking at it.
M He wanted to catch it and take it home.

25 Where does this story take place

A In a toy store
B In a park
C In a school room
D In a zoo

Section 1

Frida Kahlo was born in Mexico in 1907. At school she trained to be a scientist. But then came the accident that changed her life. A streetcar struck the bus that she was riding in.

For months, Frida had to stay in bed. In the hospital, she had nothing to do. She couldn't even leave her bed. So she set up a mirror and painted a picture of her face. She found that she loved to paint.

Section 2

Soon afterwards, she met Diego Rivera. Rivera was a famous Mexican artist. Frida showed Diego her work. He liked it, and he liked Frida even more. Soon they were married. Frida was madly in love with her husband. She cared more about Diego than anything else. They shared a tremendous love of life, of people, of gossip, of animals, of Mexico, of politics, of art.

Frida began to paint more and more. Her favorite subject was herself. A typical Frida painting shows her with her hair piled high on her head. Her dark eyebrows meet above her nose. She is dressed in an old-fashioned Mexican costume. In the background of her paintings, she put her pet monkeys and parrots.

Section 3

Frida loved to explore Mexico. At one point, she became an art teacher. Her lessons were unusual. She led her students out of the classroom to all sorts of places. They went to ancient Mexican pyramids, to markets, to factories, and to the countryside. Everywhere, Frida urged her students to mix with the local people.

Section 4

After she turned 35, Frida became very sick. She spent most of her time in hospitals or lying flat on her back in her bed at home. She and Diego often painted quick little works and sold them just to pay the doctors' bills. She died the following year, but her paintings have become famous all over the world.

26 **What would be a good title for this passage?**

J "A Wasted Life"
K "Mexican Art"
L "The Life and Art of Diego Rivera"
M "The Life and Art of Frida Kahlo"

27 **In Section 2, why did Frida use a mirror when she painted?**

A To be able to look through the window
B To see if her face had been damaged by the accident
C To see what her face looked like
D To see the other patients in the ward

28 **Which picture is most likely to be a painting by Frida Kahlo?**

29 Which sentence tells you that Frida Kahlo was an exciting teacher?

    A "For months, Frida had to stay in bed."
    B "Frida loved to explore Mexico."
    C "Her favorite subject was herself."
    D "She led her students out of the classroom to all sorts of places."

30 If Frida Kahlo had not died as a young woman, what do you think would have happened to her?

    J She would have stopped painting pictures.
    K She would have become world famous while she was still alive.
    L She would have begun to paint pictures of streets and houses.
    M She would have moved to the United States.

31 What would you guess about Diego Rivera from this passage?

    A He loved his wife very much.
    B He was jealous of his wife.
    C He loved Mexico.
    D He thought art was more important than people.

32 When the author writes about "a typical Frida painting," this means

    J a painting that Frida and Diego painted together.
    K the time of day that Frida usually painted.
    L the kind of painting Frida usually painted.
    M the kind of paints Frida used.

33 What do you think the writer thought of Frida Kahlo?

    A He thought she was a bad teacher and a bad artist.
    B He thought she was a complicated person but a lot of fun.
    C He thought she should have cared for her husband more.
    D He thought she lived a lonely, unhappy life.

PREPARATION FOR THE IOWA TEST OF BASIC SKILLS® GRADE 3 READING COACH
TEACHER'S GUIDE & ANSWER KEY

Description of the Test

Educational Design's **ITBS Coach** is designed to prepare Chicago's Elementary School students for the Reading Comprehension portion of the third-grade **Iowa Test of Basic Skills** ("ITBS").

The **ITBS Reading Comprehension Test** includes a wide variety of selections drawn from many narrative and informational genres, including biography, fables and poems, diary entries, short stories, and scientific and historical passages. The **ITBS Coach** mirrors the test's variety of subject matter.

The test asks questions at three different levels: factual recall, inferential meaning, and evaluative meaning. The **Coach** also divides reading strategies and skills into these three different levels. Approximately 20% of the questions are answered by factual recall; the remainder require students to use higher-order thinking skills.

Content and Organization

Part 1: Factual Meaning

1. Recalling Stated Information
   Sequence
2. Working Out What Words Mean
   Phrases

Part 2: Inferential and Interpretive Meaning

3. Making Inferences and Drawing Conclusions
   Setting
4. Making Generalizations and Applying
   Information
   Using a Pictorial Format
   Predicting Outcomes
5. Describing and Analyzing Characters in
   Stories
   Comparing Characters

Part 3: Evaluative Meaning

6. Finding Main Ideas, Topics, and Themes
7. Identifying the Author's Viewpoint and
   Purpose
8. Interpreting Figurative Language

Each chapter begins with an overview of a particular learning outcome, which is then taught by examples and feedback. Students then learn *Strategies and Tips* for answering questions requiring the use of this skill. Chapters end with practice selections and questions. These questions use the language employed on the **ITBS Test**.

Part 4 of **The Coach** consists of two complete Practice Tests. Students read between seven and ten passages and answer multiple-choice questions based on them—approximately the same number of questions as the test contains.

Practice Test 1 can be used diagnostically. Answer Feedback follows the test. The answers to Practice Test 2 and to the practice selections can be found in this Teacher's Guide.

Teaching Strategy

Many teachers prefer to use **The Coach** in a classroom setting, working either with the whole class or with smaller groups of students. When used in this manner, teachers begin with the instructional units in Parts One, Two, and Three of the **Coach** and cover each chapter in sequence. The teacher often introduces each unit at the beginning of the period and goes through the examples, allowing adequate time for classroom discussion. Then the students complete the selections individually or in groups and the class discusses their answers. Most teachers use about one classroom period per instructional unit.

© EDUCATIONAL DESIGN, INC., 345 HUDSON STREET, NEW YORK, NY, 10014

Answer Key

Chapter 1		Chapter 5		Practice Test 2	
1.	D	1.	B	1.	B
2.	B	2.	D	2.	J
3.	C	3.	C	3.	C
4.	C	4A.	B	4.	J
5.	C	4B.	D	5.	B
6.	A			6.	M
Chapter 2		**Chapter 6**		7.	C
1.	C	1.	C	8.	L
2.	A	2.	C	9.	B
3.	B	3.	D	10.	K
4.	D	4A.	D	11.	B
5.	B	4B.	A	12.	L
6.	D			13.	D
Chapter 3		**Chapter 7**		14.	M
1.	C	1.	A	15.	C
2.	C	2.	A	16.	K
3.	C	3A.	A	17.	D
		3B.	D	18.	K
Chapter 4		4A.	D	19.	C
1.	B	4B.	C	20.	K
2.	A			21.	D
3.	D	Chapter 8		22.	K
		1.	B	23.	B
		2A.	C	24.	L
		2B.	A	25.	B
		2C.	B	26.	M
		3.	B	27.	C
				28.	L
				29.	D
				30.	K
				31.	A
				32.	L
				33.	B

EDUCATIONAL DESIGN, INC.